Book 1 in the Land to Lots™ Trilogy

Fields to Fortune

PLANNING YOUR BIGGER FUTURE

A Step-by-Step Guide for Leveraging
The Launch Sequence™ in Your Next Master
Planned Community

Other Books by Carter Froelich

The Real Estate Wake Up Call: The Secrets to Real Estate Success

Land to Lots: How to Borrow Money You Don't Have to Pay Back and LAUNCH Master Planned Communities

Book 1 in the Land to Lots™ Trilogy

Fields to Fortune

PLANNING YOUR BIGGER FUTURE

A Step-by-Step Guide for Leveraging
The Launch Sequence™ in Your Next Master
Planned Community

CARTER FROELICH

ethos
collective

Printed in the United States of America

Published by Ethos Collective™
PO Box 43, Powell, OH 43065
www.ethoscollective.vip

LCCN: 2024911790
Paperback ISBN: 978-1-63680-334-0
Hardcover ISBN: 978-1-63680-335-7
e-book ISBN: 978-1-63680-336-4

Table of Contents

Acknowledgments

The journey from Fields to Fortune and the creation of The Launch Sequence™ wouldn't have been possible without the countless lessons learned from the talented developers and home builders I've encountered. Their insights, successes, and challenges have been invaluable in shaping the content of this book. My deepest gratitude goes out to all the contributions you have made over my forty years of working in the industry.

A Note from the Author

Fields to Fortune represents the first book in the value enhancement trilogy within the Land to Lots™ universe, which is focused on creating your bigger future through the leveraging of The Launch Sequence™.

Fields to Fortune focuses on the critical first stage of The Launch Sequence: The Planning Phase.

Now, I know what you're thinking: planning might not sound as glamorous as groundbreaking or ribbon-cutting ceremonies. But trust me, when it comes to master planned community development, a solid plan is the bedrock of your success.

Fields to Fortune is your guide to navigating this crucial first phase. We'll delve deep into the practical details of:

- The Project Vision™: What are your personal and financial goals in developing the project? What are the dangers that must be overcome, the opportunities seized, and the strengths that you and your project offer that will assist you in achieving your goals?

- Return Metrics: What are your financial goalposts? Are you internal rate of return driven or nominal dollar driven? Your choice will dictate the financing vehicle(s) utilized to finance your project's infrastructure.

- The Launch Market Driven Bond Sizing™: What is the maximum bonding capacity the project can generate based on our analysis of the surrounding competitive project's property tax rates and your project's eligible infrastructure costs?

- The RED Analysis™: What strategies can you use to Reduce, Eliminate, and/or Defer infrastructure costs?

- Financial Modeling: Crunching the numbers, how do special district financing, impact fee credits, other reimbursement vehicles, and the results of the RED Analysis impact your returns and profitability?

- The Launch Finance Plan™: Communicate your development and financing plan to jurisdictional representatives in a manner that is simple for them to understand and preliminarily approve.

By the time you finish this book, you'll have a roadmap in hand, ready to turn that raw land into a thriving development.

Remember, in the world of real estate, failing to plan is planning to fail. *Fields to Fortune* equips you with the tools and knowledge to avoid those costly missteps and set yourself up for a project that generates not just profits but lasting success.

Introduction

I would like to invite you on a journey. This is a journey from land to lots, from fields to fortune, and from mere plans to master-planned communities.

As your guide on this journey, I can offer you the expertise of over 40 years of helping people like you achieve their land development goals. My team at Launch Development Finance Advisors works with land developers, commercial developers, and home builders to finance their infrastructure using a proven process called The Launch Sequence™. The genius of The Launch Sequence is that it enables our clients to borrow money to finance infrastructure in such a way that it is paid back by the end users of the project. In essence, you get to borrow money you don't have to pay back.

It almost sounds too good to be true, doesn't it?

The good news is that the whole process is laid out in my first book, *Land To Lots: How to Borrow Money You Don't Have to Pay Back and LAUNCH Master Planned Communities.* You'll get the whole vision and possibility of the process there. If you're already convinced, though, keep reading.

This book is the beginning of a three-part value enhancement series. I will break down The Launch Sequence into its stages and discuss the practical elements of each. This means that you get to see the fine details of the process and you get the tools to start applying it to your own master-planned community dreams.

What Is The Launch Sequence™?

When starting a real estate project, the details can be overwhelming. Every goal can mire you in endless considerations and scenario planning. The Launch Sequence is our solution, and we will be with you every step of the way on your journey from land to lots.

We specialize in taking our client's development and financing goals, breaking them down, and laying out the best path and plan to help them achieve those goals.

The best part? The Launch Sequence is foolproof. It works all the time. In every situation. In every state. For every client.

So how does it work? Fundamentally, every developer starts with a jigsaw puzzle box. Inside are their goals, challenges, and opportunities, but they are all puzzle pieces jumbled together. We take that box and dump it out on the table. From there, it's just a matter of sorting the puzzle pieces by color, shape, and image as we get a feel for the size and possibility of the project. In other words, we find out where the client wants to go and what tools we have at our disposal based on the specific state and jurisdiction to help our client complete their vision.

There are three stages to The Launch Sequence:

- The Planning Process
- The Implementation Process
- The Management Process

Every project must undergo rigorous planning before it can be expertly implemented and diligently managed. Planning makes the difference between success and failure. This is even truer for long-term land development, where the stakes are high and the risk is great. This book will hone in on the intricacies of The Planning Process and give you every tool necessary to formulate a perfect project plan.

Why Should I Care?

Now, the alternative to The Launch Sequence is simply hiring an underwriter or financial advisor to do your special district bond (e.g., CFD, CDD, Metro, MUD, SID, PID, etc.) sizing and be done with it. I have great admiration and affection for my underwriting and financial advisor colleagues. There is no question that they are very good at what they do.

It is important to remember, however, that underwriters and financial advisors don't work for you. Yes, the underwriters are the ones that run out, issue the bonds, and get the money, and ultimately, that is the goal of any type of special district financing. The two perspectives differ, however, in that the underwriters and financial advisors typically work first for the bond buyers, then for the district or jurisdiction, and only lastly for the developer. They will necessarily see things from the perspective of issuing the largest bond possible (as they are paid based upon the par amount of the bonds) and doing so in the shortest time possible with a bond structure that allows them the easiest and fastest marketing and sales period. As such, these goals can and do often ignore the realities of developing a master planned community, changing market conditions, property tax rate considerations, construction phasing, development impact fee credits and reimbursements, and most importantly, the developer's more comprehensive financing goals and business plan.

Since I began providing professional advisory services to the private sector in the mid-1980s, I have had only one concern—that of my private sector developer clients. Neither I nor the Launch Development Financing Advisor (Launch) professionals work for underwriters, financial advisors, districts, or the public sector. We have one focus: helping our private sector development clients achieve their vision and business plan. When we implement The Launch Sequence, we genuinely want the best for our clients.

Throughout this exposition of The Planning Process, you will see many lists of questions. Take this as evidence that The Launch Sequence really is about you. It is a structure and a method, but it cannot take flight until the details of *your* project are on the launch pad.

That being said, it's time to build a rocket.

PART 1

Conceptualize

The Project Vision™

Imagine sitting down with me for a meeting. For now, I only have one all-important question: "Assuming we are meeting here again three years from today, what needs to have happened for you to feel positive about your progress on the project?" That's it. Now, I stop talking and take copious notes as you describe what success looks like for you. This is what we define as The Project Vision™.

If you can answer this question in detail, then you have already taken the first step of The Launch Sequence. How you answer this question reveals a lot about your business plan, even if you don't yet think you have a formal business plan for your project. Take a moment now to think about your answer. If you're still not quite sure how you would answer, these questions can help you put your business plan in concrete terms:

- Are you a fee developer, only taking a fee for other landowners or investors?

- Are you an investor looking to entitle the project, set up a district, and then flip it to someone else?

- Are you planning to put in off-site and in-site infrastructure and sell superpads?

- Do you have adequate and/or cost-effective equity and/or debt financing?

- Will you develop finished lots over time and sell the finished lots and commercial pads to builders or commercial users?

- Do you have flexibility in your business plan to take advantage of fluctuations in the market?

- Have you already master planned the project?

- Are you looking for market intelligence about different types of lots?

- What types of entitlements do you have or are you pursuing?

- Are you planning on establishing a special-purpose taxing district?

- Are you interested in developing a legacy for yourself or your family?

Whether your business plan sounds like one of these, a combination of several, or something completely different, you most likely already have the bones of a solid plan we can help you develop.

At this point, I become a type of expedition guide for you and your project. You have outlined your destination, so now I can lay out a plan to get you there while also letting you know the challenges that we will face on the journey. So, not only am I listening for the elements of your business plan as you talk through your project vision, but I also want to know what needs to be done over these next three years.

Once you tell me your destination of choice, I can help you get there with efficiency and certainty, yet with enough flexibility that if you want to take side trips and do extra sightseeing along the way, you have the ability to do that with your project.

Again, this first step is crucial. Ensuring that you have a clear project vision keeps the project on track and gives every step we take along the way a quantifiable sense of progress toward the overarching goal.

Takeaway: What needs to have happened in three years for you to feel positive about your progress on the project?

The Return Factor Question™

The next question in understanding The Project Vision relates to the financial metric by which you are going to judge your financial success. Is your company driven by an internal rate of return (IRR) or by nominal dollars (e.g., multiple)? This is what we refer to as The Return Factor Question and the answer to this question defines your return target.

If you are motivated by IRR, you want to generate the highest IRR possible within a certain amount of time. We can then create a mechanism that accelerates cash into your proforma as fast as possible. Many public home builders are IRR-driven. They typically want to bring in as much cash as possible early in the development process. They also prefer to avoid putting any capital up in the initial stages of development until they achieve revenue events. If we can help them attain those two things, then we can easily influence and increase their IRR.

As IRR is all about the time value of money, this needs to be considered early on. We impact IRR through three components: 1) margin, 2) velocity, and 3) duration. We can establish financial strategies that address these levers of IRR in order to ensure that you achieve your goals.[1]

On the other hand, some clients don't care about the timing. If you are nominal dollar-driven, all that matters is having the largest cash returns possible at the end of the development period. If this is you, then we won't primarily concern ourselves with the time value of money when we structure the project plan but will focus on generating the largest accumulation of cash while disregarding when these funds will be received.

These are two different ways to start assembling the puzzle of your project, and there is a straightforward, effective path for your project no matter which you choose. The clearer you can be about your expectations regarding returns as you start your project, the better we can begin to structure your financing so we can achieve your return target.

Takeaway: Is your company driven by IRR or nominal dollar?

---

[1]   For more information on IRR, please reference the Land to Lots Podcast, Episodes 52 and 53 at LandtoLots.com

The Project D.O.S. Conversation

Sometimes, the hardest part of a project is thinking through the whole process. Even though we've thought through The Project Vision, we're not done yet. Now it's time for a discussion inspired by Dan Sullivan's D.O.S Conversation® from the Strategic Coach® Program. D.O.S. stands for dangers, opportunities, and strengths. Reviewing all of these facets of your project helps to set the limits and possibilities available to us moving forward.

What are the Dangers?

We always want to acknowledge a project's dangers first. If there are any obstacles, complexities, or challenges we can immediately identify, we will have a better idea of what we need to overcome to see your project vision fulfilled.

At one point, we had a client come to us looking to acquire a large property—at least a couple thousand acres. They projected many intense uses for the area, but a major issue surfaced when we had our D.O.S Conversation. The jurisdiction in which the property was located required that our client construct a large water reclamation facility that would cost upwards of half a billion dollars.

Yes, that's right. Half a *billion with a 'b'*!

We had to restructure the entire business plan around financing this facility. The typical tools available for financing were still applicable, but we needed far more financial firepower to launch the project in this case. And that was not the only problem. We had to find wastewater capacity for the client, but they also couldn't expend all their financial resources on the wastewater treatment plant because other infrastructure was necessary for the project. In the D.O.S. meeting, we came up with a long list of questions surrounding the problem that needed answering before we could proceed any further in the planning process:

- How do we come up with half a billion dollars for the construction of the treatment facility?

- How much unrestricted funding does the municipality have to offset the costs of the facility?

- Under what conditions will the municipality agree to participate in the financing?

- How are we going to fund the remainder of the roads, water, sewer, and storm drainage necessary to sell the first phase of development parcels?

- What other financing mechanisms could be established to recoup these dollars over time?

- How can we protect the project's total effective property tax rate from impairing its marketability to third-party users?

Asking questions is the first step, but eventually, there have to be solutions. We decided to start implementing tax increment financing both from property taxes, construction sales taxes, and retail sales taxes, as well as establish a development impact fee specifically for this area of the municipality. We also implemented a conduit financing bond structured as an interest-only bond for six years that the municipality would ultimately repay in year seven. Additionally, we found that the jurisdiction had roughly $300 million in unrestricted funds that we could utilize to finance portions of these facilities. In other words, there were a lot of moving parts to incorporate to overcome this overwhelming obstacle.

But here's the kicker. We realized we could go even further than simply accounting for and minimizing the dangers of financing the water treatment plant. In this case, because we had to build the water treatment plant, we could reserve all of the capacity for our client. We built and financed it, so everybody has to come to us if they want to tap into the wastewater treatment plant, which essentially creates a monopoly and shuts down potential competition.

The very stipulation that caused the initial problem became the raw material for innovation and further opportunity. I love to find these seeds of potential in every obstacle, every complexity, and every challenge because it means that the dangers don't limit a project; they expand its borders until it is more productive and profitable than it could have been otherwise.

The other takeaway from this example is the dangers involved will always be different depending on the developer's location. This is another reason that we like to take our time with the D.O.S. Conversation and record everything the developer talks about. We're listening closely to show our clients that we understand their very specific challenges, and we can personally work to overcome them and develop tools that will incorporate the solution into an even more beneficial plan.

Again, if you went to a financial advisor or underwriter to get a bond sizing for a project like this, it would do nothing to address the root of the problem and would not add any fundamental value to the project. The Launch Sequence is designed to give you a new way to view the world so you can attain your goals.

Opportunities

What opportunities do we have to capture to help you achieve your goals in this financing project?

Opportunities are different from dangers in that they involve less problem-solving to incorporate, but taking advantage of an opportunity still requires deliberate planning and careful crafting of our financing plan.

These are the types of questions that we need to now lay out on the table:

- How have you structured your purchase from the land seller?

- Do you have access to water and sewer capacity?

- Do you have a good working relationship with the jurisdiction?

- Is the jurisdiction willing to enter into special district financing?

- Does the jurisdiction have any infrastructure that they would like you to construct as part of this project? If so, can we use this fact as a negotiating chip?

- Is your project located in a great school district?

- Are property taxes remarkably low?

- What does its ingress and egress look like?

- What is the project's location in relation to employment centers?

- Do you have strong equity and/or debt providers?

- Have you entered into letters of intent and/ or purchase and sales agreements with home builders?

Consider this potential scenario. Your project is located in the county, and the city wants to annex it to aid in the growth of its property tax base. One of the things that we may do to take advantage of this opportunity is prepare a fiscal impact analysis of what the project is going to generate if it goes into the city. That way, we have an understanding of the revenue the city is going to collect over time, and we can feasibly arrange to use some of that revenue to finance our infrastructure.

Once we have this information, we will start negotiating with our legal team to prepare a pre-annexation and development agreement (PADA). This can determine how much of the city's revenue we can put toward your project. We generally overload the PADA with very favorable financing language, meaning we are going to create certainty that the jurisdiction will establish the special district as a part of the annexation.

Built into the PADA is some sort of clawback mechanism to protect your investment in case the jurisdiction decides they do not want to form the district for whatever reason. If the district is not established, we will have it in writing either that the jurisdiction will construct certain infrastructure or that we can de-annex from the city. Either way, we will have some mechanism to make it painful for the city if they back out on what they said they would do as a part of the pre-annexation and development agreement.

A PADA can often be a key instrument when assessing and harnessing the annexation opportunities of your project. As it relates to financing infrastructure through a special district, you will want to consider the following:

- How will the governance of the district be run?
- How will the district consultant's underwriters be selected?
- Who will select them?
- What facilities will be financed through the district?
- How will it be financed (special assessment, general obligation, and/or revenue bonds)?
- What is the anticipated target ad valorem tax rate for the issuance of general obligation bonds?
- What is the most advantageous value-to-lien ratio we can establish for the use of special assessment bonds?
- Do we have the ability to use special district bond proceeds to build out of bond proceeds?
- To the extent we are funding development impact fee-eligible infrastructure through the district, what are our estimated development impact fee credits?
- What type of funding contributions might be made by the jurisdiction, and when will those contributions be made?

Amid all these considerations, we want to create the largest reasonable shopping basket possible so that you can pick and choose the best possible combination of infrastructure and financing methods.

In addition to special districts, there are other financing mechanisms to consider, such as tax increment financing (TIF), which includes sales and property taxes. We may also ask the city or jurisdiction to contribute to financing certain infrastructure from their general fund, or it might be appropriate to require and document that they *will* construct certain infrastructure.

To the extent that they have development impact fees, we want to make sure that either we're setting up a specific service area so that we're collecting fees that benefit our project only and they're not running to benefit some other part of the city. If others have better development impact fee rates and we don't have our own service area, we want to make sure that we're getting "favored nation" status among developers. In that case, we would benefit from that better development impact fee rate as well.

Again, there are so many things we can include in a PADA to make sure you get the deal you want. We have effective, predetermined language that we can put into the PADA. In our 40+ years of experience working with developers, jurisdictions, and/or legal colleagues, we have learned exactly what specific language works in a PADA to achieve the desired result.

This language can be included in not only the PADA but also your standard development agreements and other special district financing-related agreements.

Sometimes, the opportunities for your project are less obvious. You might often see an underwriter or financial advisor provide a limit for your financing that does not maximize your opportunities, especially when it comes to property tax. They might say that the maximum you can do for your financing is x number of dollars in equivalent ad valorem property taxes.

I've seen this often in the Southwest. We had one instance, a project called Verrado, in Buckeye, Arizona. Half of Verrado was in the Saddleback Mountain School District, and that school district included the Palo Verde nuclear plant. As a result of the nuclear plant being included within the boundaries of the school district, the district had a very low ad valorem property tax.

As a part of this process, we were looking to annex Verrado into the city of Buckeye. Now, the underwriters and developers said to keep the ad valorem property tax no higher than $3 per $100 of assessed valuation because that's what everyone else in the area was doing. We decided to look at the situation differently. We postulated we could increase the ad valorem property tax to $10 and still be competitive with the surrounding marketplace. That extra $10 financing that we included in our PADA would make the financing worth more than what the property ultimately sold for.

As a result, we did move forward with the community facilities district. Our client did not raise the tax all the way to $10, although that was included in their annexation agreement. They decided to raise it to only $7, but that still made a huge impact on our client's pro forma, and they were able to create a very special place.

The Launch Sequence specializes in identifying opportunities like this one and using them to create the most possible value for clients and their projects.

Strengths

Finally, the D.O.S. Conversation addresses the strengths of your company, employees, consultants, and your specific project. As we lay out the puzzle pieces of your project, we are now looking for the boldest colors and the clearest images. What stands out about you or your organization that we can support or reinforce to help you achieve your three-year goals?

There are three strength areas we like to talk through with clients. The first involves looking back on their past experience and how it gives them an edge over the competition. If you ask the following questions, what comes to the forefront about your experience?

- How many communities have you developed over the years?

- What are your best relationships with local jurisdictions, and why have your relationships been so positive and collaborative?

- With which builders do you have the best relationships and what has happened over the years to cultivate these relationships?

- Tell me about your greatest successes in developing a community. Why were these considered a success?

- What are residents and community leaders saying about your communities?

Next, we look at team dynamics. Who are you working with, and what strengths do they bring to the table that can be maximized?

- Describe the talent on your team. What makes each person stand out?

- How long have team members been with your company, and what offers does your company provide to keep the team members so engaged?

- Do you have an internal team, or do you rely on external consultants to build your community?

- Who are your external team members, and how long have you been working together?

- What special talents do your external team members bring to the table?

Finally, what are your strengths regarding financing itself? We are looking here to pin down your mode of operation when it comes to financing so that the process is as seamless as possible.

- Tell me about the best financing structure you have done. What made the transaction so effective?

- Who are the financing sources you go to again and again for financing (both debt and equity)? Describe the relationship with these institutions.

- What financing options do these institutions provide that others do not?

- Describe the most impactful special districts your company created and why this structure was so beneficial for the project and your company.

The more we know about where you're coming from and what assets you already possess, the better we can help you formulate and execute a plan tailored to your unique strengths. The best part about this process is how our clients gain independence as we help them leverage their strengths.

During the strength portion of our conversation with one of our public builder clients, they revealed a wealth of inherent strengths. They had deep ties with the community, a fantastic bench of talent, and tons of cash on hand. The only advantage they lacked was a team experienced in special district financing.

This client asked if we would function as their "internal special district financing department." We gladly accepted this offer and began to work with the division to utilize their strengths and establish their goals.

We established multiple financing districts and issued special assessment bonds to fund the construction of roads, water, sewers, and storm drainage facilities. We also worked with their land development, contracting, and accounting teams and their engineering firm to determine which costs to finance with districts and how to prepare plan sets for contracting. We created standardized procurement manuals for bidding (Design, Bid, Build; Design Build; and Construction Manager at Risk), established special district job costing and cost code, and developed processes to allow Launch to track their reimbursable costs and backup using the Launch Reimbursement System (LRS).

Over time and through our interactions with our clients' teams, they became more and more confident, to the point that they effectively took over every role related to special district financing, with the exception of tracking and processing reimbursements through the LRS. We had, in fact, worked ourselves out of a job, which is exactly what we set out to do when beginning a strengths conversation.

Takeaway: What are the dangers, opportunities, and strengths inherent in your company, and how can you best leverage them?

PART 2

Customize

Preparing The Eligible Cost and Fee Analysis™

Now that we can survey all these puzzle pieces of information we laid out during the D.O.S. Conversation, we need to pinpoint exactly what the costs are going to be and how we might deal with each one. As you obtain probable costs and fee estimates from the engineers, we can start to review all of them and work them into our project plan.

There is always a plethora of moving pieces surrounding the construction of infrastructure. When we sort through the listing of infrastructure projects, we're looking for options, so we list every potential infrastructure project that could be financed via special districts, development impact fees, jurisdiction, property tax increment, reimbursement agreements, and other potential municipal financing mechanisms. That way, we can pick and choose what facilities we want to finance with what type of reimbursement vehicle to allow us to accelerate reimbursements and/or generate the largest reimbursement amount over time. We do that by making sure we have listed every possible soft cost, hard cost, financing cost, and real property interest as being eligible for reimbursement so long as that is allowed by that particular state's enabling legislation.

It is always important to have a degree of clarity when planning a project, but it is especially critical in this case to understand exactly what we have to finance. Many of these costs are items we will have to ask jurisdiction to allow, especially regarding the formation of special districts or other financing mechanisms.

Once we have the listing of costs, we prepare The Cost Segregation Analysis™. This is where we start matching facilities to their financing methods. The options for funding include special taxing districts, reimbursement agreements, development impact fees, line extension agreements, and more. Some types of infrastructure could even be funded by the jurisdiction or agency, and some may lend themselves to cost-sharing agreements with other benefiting landowners.

As a real-life example of a cost-sharing agreement, we started working on a project with one landowner. The project involved building a huge sewer interceptor line that would run from the northern part of the jurisdiction to the southern part, where the wastewater treatment plant was located. We found no fewer than twelve other landowners who would also benefit from this sewer interceptor line.

We then came up with a mechanism to distribute the cost of the project between all the landowners involved and allocate them to the benefiting lands.

Initially, we established that the cost-sharing mechanism would be based on each developer's planned Equivalent Development/Dwelling Unit (EDU), but we quickly ran into a problem. All the developers' planned EDUs ranged from a number X to a higher number Y. Although we estimated costs based on the higher numbers, each developer shifted their units around to reflect the lower numbers to avoid some of the costs of the sewer interceptor line. Once we realized what was happening, we scrapped that mechanism and instead used gross acreage to allocate costs, assuming three and a half EDUs per acre.

If you needed to create a cost-sharing agreement for a project, it would likely follow a similar methodology. Since that misjudgment happened, we always allocate costs based on a consistent factor among every landowner or developer involved.

Once we determined a foolproof cost-sharing mechanism for the sewer interceptor line project, we worked with attorneys to prepare the actual agreement and budgets for each party involved. Everyone knew exactly what they would have to pay and when they would pay it.

We monitored these budgets, making sure draws were allocated according to everyone's cost-sharing methodology. We also ensured the money actually came in and that the contractors were paid.

Our other responsibility regarding the coordination of this cost-sharing agreement was to protect each contributor's investment. We view the construction as being intended for those who invest in it and for them only. As a result, if anyone besides the contributors wants to tap in and utilize the line, they would pay a hefty financial penalty because they didn't initially join the cost-sharing agreement. This stipulation preserves the capacity of the sewer interceptor line and rewards those who have backed the project from the beginning.

This example gives you a feel for how cost-sharing agreements can operate. It also provides insight into how we can coordinate and manage different financing methods once we know what your goals and capabilities are.

There are a few more financing options that usually make it onto The Cost Segregation Analysis: construction and transaction privilege taxes, property tax increment, and also jurisdictional contributions for oversizing.

If we only need a 12-inch line in a certain project, but the jurisdiction wants a 24-inch line, then we can ask them to cover the oversizing cost. Since we're in the ground anyway, we've incurred trenching costs, but if the jurisdiction can pay for the incremental oversizing costs, we don't have to worry about the incremental cost or about waiting to be reimbursed over time. I make it a practice to always stipulate in development agreements that the developer is only responsible for constructing the improvements necessary to serve their project, and if the jurisdiction wants to upsize the facilities, the incremental costs are their financial responsibility.

These are most of the mechanisms available to you as you consider the different costs associated with your project. Your options are abundant, but no matter how we help you structure the project, we will always work to find innovative ways to finance your infrastructure and create new revenue streams.

Once we've entered every possible cost or fee into The Cost Segregation Analysis and ensured they are allocated to an achievable financing method, we can identify what we need to discuss with the jurisdiction.

What Am I Missing?

It is easy to overlook a lot of eligible infrastructure. Because it is always better to have more options, let's go over a few of those potentialities that are commonly missed. Do remember, though, that these vary widely from state to state. For instance, in some states, California being one, we can even finance school fees and jurisdictional impact fees. I believe there is a good chance we can finance these types of facilities in a lot of other states because the infrastructure that is financed by impact fees is all public, and the jurisdiction created a rational nexus study when it prepared its impact fee study. We're having those conversations right now with other states as we try to move the concept from California to other places, which could broaden the horizons for so many looking at their eligible infrastructure costs, including impact fees.

We can also purchase rights of way, easements, and other real property interests, so we want to make sure that they are eligible for financing and/or reimbursement as well. We can purchase easements through a special district and then provide these real property interests at no cost to the jurisdiction, district, or other quasi-public entity. This is a great way to "recapitalize" your land costs. You might also consider adding the ability to get paid financing costs. To the extent that you're funding out of capital and waiting for the jurisdiction and/or special district to reimburse you, we want to make sure you're being paid for financing costs, as this is a real cost of the project.

Again, we're examining all of the different costs involved and putting them all together for your ease so that you can have the largest "shopping basket" full of possibilities to choose from. As we begin to segregate those costs into various cost groupings, we start to have a better understanding of how we're going to finance the various facilities and how all of these financing mechanisms are going to coalesce.

Takeaway: List every potential cost, then match each cost to a financing/reimbursement mechanism.

Research and Prepare The Launch Competitive Tax Rate Analysis™

The next item that is hugely important to your project is looking at your property tax rate vis-á-vis the competition. Even though we know our development costs and what costs are potentially eligible for financing through the special district, we still begin our special district financing with the property's current property tax rate. At this phase in the planning process, we research and prepare The Launch Competitive Tax Rate Analysis, and like every other phase, we begin by asking questions.

- What is your current property tax rate?

- How will your special district tax/assessment increase your project's ad valorem property tax rate equivalent?

- Do your conditions of approval require the joining of fire, water, or maintenance districts? If so, how will this impact your total effective property tax rate?

- If you're in the county or the extra-territorial jurisdiction and you're annexing into a jurisdiction, what will be the impact on the tax rate once you annex into the jurisdiction?

- What are the competitive effective property tax rates of your competitive development projects?

We at Launch will always arrange the most flexible special district financing possible, but if we don't take into account the effective ad valorem property tax rates of the competitive supply and load up our clients' property tax rate so that it is dramatically higher than the competition, then home builders and home buyers may be driven away from purchasing our client's project. People will always vote with their dollars. If our project's effective property tax rate is out of sync with the competition, we risk impairing our project's marketability with home builders and buyers.

We need to know the competitive marketplace's tax rate so we can build the best financing structure possible. When home buyers are buying, it ought to be clear to them that, all things being equal, the property taxes in our client's master plan community are comparable to the competition's.

Suppose our property tax rate is significantly higher than the surrounding communities. In that case, we need to have some very specific, tangible things we can point out to show why the home-buying population should be willing to pay more to be in our project versus someone else's. To this end, we want to be able to point to specific infrastructure items and show builders and home buyers what we have financed through the special district and/or the financing arrangement structure in the PADA or development agreement, such as:

- Impressive entrance monumentation
- Public schools
- Public parks
- Open space
- Walking trails
- Bike paths
- Hiking/walking trails
- Public gathering spaces for concerts/food trucks/farmer's markets
- Amenity centers with pools, splash pads, pickleball, and tennis courts
- Crystal lagoons

It also helps to know the development impact fees the competitive master plans are paying. If we have competition in different counties or nearby cities, they will have different impact fees that they have to pay. It is important to know the total impact fees that builders will have to pay as this will impact the price at which they can purchase the property. Secondly, it is important to know what public infrastructure is eligible for financing and/or reimbursement with impact fees, as these facts will impact the amount of funding competitive developers can pursue as it relates to their competitive projects.

Furthermore, one should understand what homeowner's association (HOA) dues are being charged by the competitive developments and what the HOA dues are being used for. At the end of the day, potential new home buyers can only afford a finite payment, and in addition to the cost of the monthly mortgage payment, property taxes, property insurance, and HOA dues factor into the mortgage qualification process. All of this information can help inform us and lead us down one path or another.

We do all this to ensure that your project is competitive. But there is another benefit of taking such a deep dive into your project's competition. When your project is the only one you think about for months on end, it is easy to become enamored, and rightfully so. I have worked with clients on some truly gorgeous master planned communities over the years. I want to caution you, though. Don't get so wrapped up in your own project that you forget how it relates to the competitive environment. At this point, it pays to look clear-eyed at the numbers. We can help by giving you an unbiased interpretation of what the numbers are saying and what those opportunities and challenges will be if we keep our tax rates comparable to our competition. Again, if we decide that we can reasonably exceed the property tax rates of the competition, the homeowners need to feel that they are getting great value for their money. We need to provide them with a justifiable benefit, such as

- Great location
- Great school district based on ratings and test scores
- Best ingress and egress to transportation corridors
- The only project with topography or views in the area
- The last developable parcel in the city
- Natural or manmade amenities that no nearby community possesses
- Fantastic physical amenities and soft programming

We need to be so practical and honest with ourselves. One of the worst traps to fall into is overburdening a project with excessive and unjustifiable special district taxes that homeowners will have to bear.

Takeaway: Look at the competition and make sure you can keep your project competitive.

Prepare The Launch Market Driven Bond Sizing™

Now that we understand what property tax rate we can increase our property taxes to, we use this information along with the response to The Return Factor Question (i.e., Are you IRR-driven or nominal dollar-driven?).

We understand our eligible infrastructure costs and fees by preparing The Eligible Cost and Fee Analysis. We've got our Launch Competitive Tax Rate Analysis and know the property tax rates of the competitive supply. Now, we take all this information and drop it into The Launch Market Driven Bond Sizing.

Depending on what state we're in, this process is going to look different. Here are a few examples to give you a sense of the variety of different bond types we can issue:

- In California, it's a bond secured by a special tax levy.
- In Arizona, we look at general obligation bonds and special assessment bonds.
- In Nevada, it's a special assessment bond.
- In Idaho, it's a combination of general obligation and special assessment bonds.
- In Florida, its special assessment bonds.
- In Texas, if it's a PID, it's a special assessment bond. If it's an MMD, it's a general obligation bond and/or a special assessment bond, or if it's a MUD, it's a general obligation bond.

We also have the ability in Texas to layer on a tax increment reinvestment zone (TIRZ), which is a city and/or county property tax increment. So, every state is a little different.

In essence, the best type of bond for the project varies based on our client's Project Vision, return target, state, jurisdiction, and special district type.

Special Assessment Bonds

The ideal choice if you are IRR-driven is special assessment (SA) bonds.

It's not possible in every situation, but when it is, an SA bond can be incredibly financially efficient in the development process. It allows us to issue SA bonds off of the land's fair market value, provided that the infrastructure to be financed through the SA bonds and any other infrastructure for which completion guarantees have been provided is in place as of the date of valuation.

We are then issuing off of either a 2:1 or 3:1 value-to-lien ratio. For example, if the fair market value of each lot is $75,000 and we are issuing SA bonds assuming a 3:1 value-to-lien ratio, we are able to secure $25,000 per lot ($75,000/3) to fund infrastructure. We will either be able to get that money and build out of bond proceeds, or we will be able to get that money sooner in the process to reimburse us for the cost of the infrastructure we just constructed. Remember, SA bonds allow us to increase the velocity of bond proceeds, thereby allowing us to impact the IRR favorably.

As with most of these processes so far, you have options. Based on what we've learned from our experiences, we have created universal templates for SA bond sizings. We have learned that in Florida, for example, we can have an "A" bond and a "B" bond. The A bond is long-term and will be passed on to the homeowner. Because we have so much value in the land, we may do a secondary bond. This is called the B bond, and it is typically a 5-year, short-term bond.

We utilize the A/B bond structure when we have significant value in the land and we want to maximize the tax-exempt, non-recourse bond financing proceeds to construct infrastructure. Assuming we have tremendous value in the land but know that the homeowners will only accept a certain level of special assessment lien on their property, we utilize the A/B bond structure to maximize construction proceeds. We load up the property with the maximum lien possible, with the idea of only passing on the A bond, which is secured by the special assessment lien that the market will bear. We can assess the B bond, which is the difference between the A bond and the maximum, via the value-to-lien requirements. Once we have a revenue event, such as the sale of the lot to a home builder or buyer, we pay off the B bond and pass off the A bond. The B bond is, in essence, mezzanine financing for the project.

What will that do for us?

For one thing, we will not have so much equity involved in the development process. We are building out bond proceeds using other people's money, and again, as soon as we have a revenue event, we pay off the B bond, and the A bond goes to the homeowner.

Formats like this one can be helpful in your own planning process, but this only begins to inform what we are trying to do. You cannot structure financing solely by running a bond sizing. You have to understand everything on the table and how the pieces come together, and that's what Launch does through The Project Vision and The D.O.S. Conversation.

Sometimes, in Texas, we will attempt to maximize SA bonds using a TIRZ subsidy. We will use that subsidy to pay down our assessment. This allows us to issue an SA bond that is larger than that which would otherwise be available; however, to keep the homeowner payment reasonable, we'll use the TIRZ subsidy collected by the county to pay down the annual assessment to the home as it gets on the county property tax rolls, and as the city and the county give us portions of their property tax revenue.

The homeowner pays a market-driven effective tax property rate, but some of that payment comes from revenue that they pay the city and county, which the city and county then pay back to us to pay down the tax rate to an acceptable level for the marketplace.

Again, the feasibility of these methods depends on the jurisdiction, but we have proven methods for your specific situation.

The only drawback to SA bonds is that they are "one and done." We issue a special assessment lien on a property and then sell the property, and the process ends there. We typically never issue another special assessment on that property. This is not ideal if you are nominal dollar-driven. Luckily, there's a perfect solution.

General Obligation Bonds

General obligation (GO) bonds are for those who aren't as concerned about the time value of money, provided they receive the maximum amount of reimbursement for infrastructure from the project.

With GO bonds, we can issue debt over and over again, and as we issue those GO bonds, the interest rate typically goes down over time as we have diversified the risk to the bond buyers from one master developer to multiple home builders and hundreds or thousands of homeowners. Additionally, we're able to issue new GO bonds every year as well as refinance older bonds as we sell more homes and/or existing home values within the district increase over time.

So what exactly does that mean?

Let's look at an example. Say we have a Texas MUD and are levying $0.90 for debt service. The first bond issue we do would be at a higher interest rate because those bonds have not yet been rated. We're at the riskiest stage of the transaction (i.e., the beginning). All the repayment responsibility is with the master developer and maybe a handful of home builders. That first bond may be relatively small in size, somewhere in the range of $500,000. It's secured by the $0.90 ad valorem tax rate. Over time, we have more builders in our project, building more homes, and we've diversified the repayment risk from one master developer and a couple of home builders to now a master developer, multiple home builders, and hundreds of home buyers. The risk profile on that transaction has gone down, and the interest rate, which might have initially been at 5%, has now dropped to 4% as the project has a proven tax record and multiple parties to pay the debt service on the GO bonds.

Not only do we have a higher assessed valuation from more homes being constructed, but over time, as homes are constructed, their prices go up. This impacts the assessed valuations of the existing homes on the property tax roles, which creates greater assessed valuations and, in turn, allows us to issue more GO bonds.

As the GO bond interest rates are going down, we're able to refinance the old 5% debt to 4% debt, which enables us to withdraw more money over time to reimburse us for eligible costs.

That's the beauty of the GO bonds. Unlike the special assessment bond, we can revisit the GO bond almost endlessly, issuing more debt, lowering the interest rates further, and using that revenue to repay us over time.

One of the pros of the GO bond is that we can issue multiple debt instruments over time as the assessed valuation increases, as we diversify the risk, and as we can refinance the old outstanding bonds.

The major con of the GO bond is we have to wait longer in the pro forma for us to be able to get that money. So, if the time value of money influences you, you should look instead at the special assessment bonds where we can get that money sooner in the process. With this said, in the state of Texas, we did create a new financing mechanism called the MUD Forward Funding Launch Bond™, which allows us to "forward fund" future MUD bond receipts and accelerate the receipt of these reimbursements into the cash flow.[2]

Takeaway: Are SA or GO bonds better suited for your project based on availability and return target?

---

[2] For more information on the Launch Bond see TheLaunchBond.com.

Perform The RED Analysis™

So far, we have laid out the puzzle pieces of your project, sorted them, and arranged them in the best possible way to make it easy to begin assembling them. In other words, we have

- Determined eligible costs
- Identified the available types of financing
- Performed a cost segregation analysis
- Compared property tax rates to the competition
- Estimated potential bonding capacity through tax levies, SA bonds, and/or GO bonds

Now, we can perform The RED Analysis, which means we look at how we can **R**educe, **E**liminate, and **D**efer construction costs. Essentially, we are now taking our puzzle and determining whether there are any places we can simplify the project's infrastructure requirements without sacrificing any value.

Reduce

At this point, we will look at costs, conditions of approval, phasing maps and construction schedules, cross sections, and maps of the infrastructure location. With every infrastructure item under review, we ask what costs we can reduce.

For instance, whenever a jurisdiction wants our client to build something like a wastewater treatment plant, they tend to ask for the Rolls-Royce of all treatment plants. Their first request will always have more bells and whistles than is reasonable because they don't have to pay for it. If there is another checkbook they can look at, they want us to build the finest wastewater treatment plant available, given the technology at the time.

When we ask about reducible costs, it helps to revisit the absolute necessities involved in each infrastructure item. When a jurisdiction asks for a wastewater treatment plant, it fundamentally just needs a facility that can treat sewage and wastewater with the capability to reuse it as non-potable water or as a resource to refill aquifers.

These functions require a Toyota level of a facility, not a Rolls-Royce. This is the "reduce" conversation that we have in order to limit cost requirements. No reduction will ever inhibit functionality, but it will cut down on the frills that can easily compound unnecessary costs.

One time, we had a developer who needed to expand a wastewater treatment plant. The city wanted them to fund a $48 million facility expansion. That's a big number for any one developer to shoulder. We were able to bring in other landowners to establish a large, noncontiguous special district, and then we issued special assessment bonds and financed this wastewater treatment plant. Each of the 25 other landowners picked up their pro rata share of the cost, and we were able to solve that problem for our client by spreading the cost of the wastewater treatment plant to 24 other landowners.

In this case, we were able to reduce the cost to our client from $48 million by involving other landowners. There might be simpler solutions in other cases, but there is almost always some way to reduce costs.

Eliminate

Now, let's take it one step further. What elements of the infrastructure plan can we completely eliminate?

To help illustrate this step of The RED Analysis, let me tell you the story of the one and only time I got kicked out of a transaction. For context, this occurred before the Great Recession of 2005. The developer wanted us to issue a $120 million bond upfront to finance the project's off-site and on-site infrastructure. They planned to sell all five thousand lots in five years.

Now, $120 million is a big bond, and it can be extremely risky if the lots don't sell well. We proposed a counter-plan. We suggested to our client that they phase the bond issuances just in case we couldn't get all five thousand lots sold in five years. The developer felt strongly that we did not understand his Vision, so he threw us out of the transaction. I mean it . . . he actually kicked us out of his office.

After three years, we were brought back into the project. The original developer had lost the property, and the builders now owned it. They brought us on to restructure the district on which the developer had indeed issued a $120 million SA bond. Once we were back in the transaction, the first thing on our agenda was to identify what facilities we could eliminate.

As part of the development agreement with the city, the city wanted to be known as the "park capital" of the state. They included requirements for 30 volleyball courts, 32 basketball courts, 22 tennis courts, 8 baseball fields, and 14 multipurpose fields. We found this to be complete overkill. Not only were these amenities a lot for any one development, but it was a regional facility and the cost of this in 2005 was $57.9 million.

The project's original goal was to provide meaningful recreational facilities for the community. We could still accomplish that with fewer facilities, so we renegotiated the development agreement. We brought the recreational elements of the development agreement from a cost of $57.9 million down to $19.2 million to be funded over time, which was a reduction of 68% of the costs. This is what we mean when we ask if there are any projects and/or costs that can be eliminated. Are there physical components of the project that are extraneous or otherwise non-essential that can be eliminated to reduce costs?

Defer

Finally, we ask, "If there is nothing to reduce and nothing to eliminate, then is there at least anything we can put off for a time?"

Often, we will have a client come to us entirely overwhelmed by pressure from the city. For instance, maybe the city is pushing for a four or six-lane divided arterial road to be finished upfront when the client may not even have their model complex open.

Our job, then, is to go to the jurisdiction and barter a bit. Our traffic counts usually don't require all four lanes yet, and the city doesn't care. They just want the road. We will tell the city we will dedicate the right of way for a four-lane divided arterial, but for right now, we're only going to be building two lanes. As the traffic counts increase and as our traffic studies justify more lanes, we'll add on until we work up to the four stipulated lanes. That's where we're able to defer costs into the future. It helps anytime we don't need to commit as much money upfront in our pro forma, which impacts our IRR and reduces peak capital requirements. Instead, we stretch out costs over time so we can utilize the revenue coming in as the facilities are needed and used.

That's how to reduce, eliminate, and defer. This goes into the pro forma and impacts our nominal dollar over time.

The RED Analysis essentially provides three strategies for simplifying your project and minimizing unnecessary costs. Are there any puzzle pieces that don't necessarily belong to your specific puzzle? Will the pieces all fit together after we've reduced, eliminated, and deferred? If so, you have successfully performed The RED Analysis.

*Takeaway: **What elements of your project can you Reduce, Eliminate, and Defer?***

Prepare The Development Impact Fee Credit Analysis™

In this phase, we look at whether we need to finance any infrastructure on which the jurisdiction is collecting a development impact fee. If there is infrastructure that fits this description, there are more questions to ask:

- What is the cost of the facility in the jurisdiction's CIP?

- Is the facility a specific project or a "type of project"? That is, is it the result of an incremental expansion impact fee methodology or a planned-based impact fee methodology?

- Are we funding the specific project or similar types of projects?

- What is our impact fee credit amount? Should we collect reimbursement via the impact fee collection or pass on impact fee credits to builders?

- Which solution works best for our client's Project Vision and Return Factor Question?

We might have master developers come to us and ask if they can set up a separate service area and levy a development impact fee to offset some of the costs that they cannot finance through the special district. We can then help them devise a methodology to work with the jurisdiction to ensure that the development impact fee is enacted and the fees are collected.

At other times, we can set up private development impact fees that we collect on behalf of the master developer.

Other times, we'll be engaged by home builders and/or builder industry associations to challenge jurisdictions concerning the impact fees that they're charging.

One of these strategies might be exactly what your project needs, and if not, we will work to develop something else.

I was involved in the 2008 and 2016 updates of the National Association of Home Builders *Impact Fee Handbook*, so this is an area that we are experts in. We know how to either increase (for master planned

community developers) or decrease (for home builders) impact fees depending on who is paying us. We
can alter our plans based on whether we're receiving
impact fees that flow back in to reimburse us for infrastructure or we're passing those impact fee credits on
to the builders, which impacts the land residual. In the
end, we benefit everyone involved in the transaction.

*Takeaway: How do development impact fees affect
your project?*

Generate The Project Cash Flow Analysis™

We have set up all these great financing mechanisms, but as always, we want to be very sober in what we promise our clients we can do. Although we have had some very successful and even lucky pitches to the city, we still try to be very clear-eyed about what possibilities are feasible.

Once we have all this information to be able to run multiple what-if scenarios, we will often put this into what we call The Project Cash Flow Analysis™. This is fundamentally a test of financial sensitivity.

Our developers have very sophisticated models, but they often use a model that worked on their last project and just bring it forward, even if the projects are significantly different. Or, in the case of the builders, all they have is a template model. They're getting certain information from Launch, the underwriters, and/or financial advisors and then plugging those numbers into their pro forma. Every time they change a number, they have to run out and get a different analysis from all three parties.

As a result of this inefficiency, our clients often bring us on to incorporate all the moving parts into one functioning model. We have spent so much of the planning process discussing diverse components of the project, such as these:

- Special districts
- Cost-sharing agreements
- Reimbursement agreements
- Development impact fees
- Development impact fee credits
- Construction sales tax
- Tax increment
- Techniques to Reduce, Eliminate, or Defer Costs

We incorporate all of these into the pro forma in such a way that as our client's land use assumptions change, home prices change, or as our phasing sizes and timing change, we can show in real time the financial impacts of those changes on all our different reimbursements. With a clear picture of the possibilities, we can drill down and come up with the best financing strategy for the project. We can easily test our options so that we know what is most impactful and what is least impactful. Then, when we go into negotiations with the jurisdiction for a given project, we know that if we have to concede a request, we can know the financial impact in advance. Maybe we are willing to give those wins to the city, but they haven't run the numbers on it yet. They don't know that we are giving up the least valuable of the things we're asking for.

Having this cash flow and pro forma analysis gives us a key advantage in negotiations, especially if you are IRR-driven. We can know how every reduction, elimination, and deferment affects the time value of your money.

Takeaway: Can you easily alter your model to reflect any potential changes to the project?

PART 3

Communicate

Prepare The Project Path and Plan™

Every aspect of the project has now been duly considered. What's next? We need to record our decisions and put them in a format that is easy to understand, share, and collect feedback on.

We have reached the penultimate step in our planning process: developing The Path and Plan™ to discuss with our client. We have completed the analysis above, run the financial sensitivity analysis, and now we can meet with our client to jointly lay out a high-level roadmap of what financial tools we might discuss with the jurisdiction and other stakeholders to help our clients achieve their Project Vision.

To finalize the plan, we go through all of the different mechanisms and discuss the pros and cons of each item in The Project Path and Plan. Our clients can rate each component, either approving or refusing, lowering some estimations and raising others, choosing bond types, and so on.

With all this feedback, we are coming up with The Project Path and Plan: a holistic document that provides the clarity and flexibility to allow our clients to adjust for any changing market circumstances and conditions.

Takeaway: Can you compile all your project financing choices into one comprehensive road map?

Draft The Launch Finance Plan™ and Present to the Jurisdiction

Once we have our Path and Plan nailed down with our client, we use this framework to draft what we call The Launch Finance Plan™, a high-level written narrative representation of The Project Path and Plan. The Launch Finance Plan is the document we present to the jurisdiction as we ask them for what we need to move our project financing forward.

The Launch Finance Plan describes the project in terms of land uses, estimated units, and commercial square footage at build-out. We include estimated construction costs (in terms of total construction costs and what costs are eligible for financing through special districts), development impact fee reimbursement, reimbursement mechanisms, and what costs we would like the jurisdiction to fund, if any. We then outline what actions we would like the jurisdiction to take in terms of establishing special purpose taxing districts, what types of bonds we would like the special purpose taxing district to issue (e.g., GO bonds, SA bonds, and/or Revenue Bonds), property and/or sales tax increment requests, establishment of reimbursement districts, what projects we want the jurisdiction to finance, and the other specific things we have discussed with our client while finalizing The Project Path and Plan.

When we present The Launch Finance Plan to the jurisdiction, we introduce our client, their experience in developing master planned communities, the project, what we're doing, and what our construction timing is. We also propose what benefits to the jurisdiction we anticipate as the result of the project's development, as well as what we're asking them to do in order to partner with us and develop this community. Once we're done walking them through the financing requests outlined in The Launch Finance Plan, we can generally get a good feel for what they're going to allow us to do and what things they are not going to let us do, which we can then take off the table and group with things that will require further discussions with the jurisdiction.

We now have a clear understanding of what we can do and what we can't do. As part of The Launch

Finance Plan, we set up a schedule and assign roles and responsibilities to the developer and jurisdictional team members so that we can begin to move forward and implement what we planned during The Launch Sequence's Planning Phase. In the second book of The Land to Lots trilogy, we will discuss the steps involved in implementing The Launch Finance Plan as we continue the journey from fields to fortune.

Takeaway: Finalize your plans by drafting The Launch Finance Plan and presenting it to the jurisdiction.

Afterword

As you have learned more about how the planning process works, we hope you feel inspired to take advantage of the simplicity and clarity of the Launch Sequence. Maybe you see echoes of your own master planned community dreams in these pages of success stories.

Most likely, though, your set of dangers, opportunities, and strengths is different from anything you've heard about here. That is even more exciting! Every project is unique, and we would love to come up with new ways to leverage your D.O.S.

Regardless of where you are in your project, Launch is ready for you.

About the Author

Carter is an author and the Managing Principal of Launch Development Finance Advisors. Prior to the founding of Launch, Carter was the co-founder and Managing Principal of a national real estate consulting firm for 27 years. Preceding this, Carter was a Manager in the real estate consulting department of the national accounting firm of Kenneth Leventhal & Company in both the Phoenix, Arizona, and Newport Beach, California offices. Carter is a Certified Public Accountant in Arizona, California, and Texas, as well as a former State Certified Real Estate Appraiser in Arizona. He holds a master's degree in Real Estate

Development from the University of Southern California and a bachelor's degree in Business Economics from the University of California, Santa Barbara.

With over forty years of experience in the real estate consulting industry, Carter's area of specialty is in the formulation and implementation of land-secured financings for large-scale developments and the formulation of development strategies for large-scale master-planned communities.

Carter served as a City of Phoenix's Camelback Village Planning Committee member. He is a full member of the Urban Land Institute, Valley Partnership, and is a member of numerous Building Industry Associations in Arizona, California, Idaho, and Texas. Carter authored the 2008 and 2016 National Association of Home Builders' Impact Fee Handbook.

OUR SERVICES

Launch is a transaction based real estate consulting firm that specializes in the financing of public infrastructure that serves our clients development projects.

- Land Secured Financing
- Development Impact Fees
- Entitlement Analysis
- Cash Flow Analysis
- Development & Financing Agreement Negotiations
- Legislative Initiatives
- District Management
- Litigation Support
- Fiscal Impact Studies
- Public Bidding & Reimbursement Services

LAUNCH-DFA.COM

LAND TO LOTS™ PODCAST

LAND TO LOTS™

ACQUISITION, DEVELOPMENT & FINANCE

Carter Froelich hosts the Land to Lots™ podcast where he and his team help their clients finance infrastructure, reduce costs and mitigate risks all with the goal of enhancing project profitability.

LANDTOLOTS.COM

Enjoy The Other Books in the Land To Lots Series

 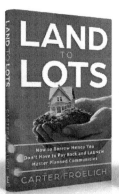 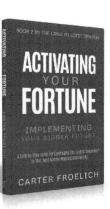

AVAILABLE WHEREVER BOOKS ARE SOLD

THIS BOOK IS PROTECTED INTELLECTUAL PROPERTY

The author of this book values Intellectual Property. The book you just read is protected by Easy IP™, a proprietary process, which integrates blockchain technology giving Intellectual Property "Global Protection." By creating a "Time-Stamped" smart contract that can never be tampered with or changed, we establish "First Use" that tracks back to the author.

Easy IP™ functions much like a Pre-Patent™ since it provides an immutable "First Use" of the Intellectual Property. This is achieved through our proprietary process of leveraging blockchain technology and smart contracts. As a result, proving "First Use" is simple through a global and verifiable smart contract. By protecting intellectual property with blockchain technology and smart contracts, we establish a "First to File" event.

Protected By Easy IP™

LEARN MORE AT EASYIP.TODAY

Made in the USA
Columbia, SC
22 November 2024

46996480R00052